CONTENTS

In Memory of Carol Schickel
1939–1991

ACKNOWLEDGMENTS

I have two large debts of gratitude to discharge. The first is to my late wife, Carol. It was she, an enthusiastic yet discerning admirer of Billy Wilder's work, who wooed me away from a certain dubiety about it, and over a decade of conversation, taught me to see it – as she taught me to see so many things – in a new light. When the editor of this series asked me to choose a title to contribute to it, it was Carol who suggested that I write about *Double Indemnity*. In the ten years we shared, she endured the writing of seven books – ever encouraging, always supportive, never – well, hardly ever – impatient. This was the last of them, and it saddens me beyond words that she did not live to read the one that was her idea. It was one of the many things that we believed – erroneously, as it turned out – there was plenty of time to do.

My other major indebtedness is to Billy Wilder himself. In the spring of 1991 he spared the time and energy for a lengthy interview about the making of *Double Indemnity*. It was everything one always hopes for (and rarely obtains) from encounters of this kind – forthright, feisty, funny. Most of the quotations attributed to Mr Wilder in this essay are drawn from that interview.

Three printed sources deserve more than cursory bibliographic acknowledgment: Roy Hoopes's *Cain*, Frank MacShane's *The Life of Raymond Chandler* and Maurice Zolotow's *Billy Wilder in Hollywood*. Without the researches of these devoted biographers it would not have been possible for me to write in as much detail as I have about *Double Indemnity*.

Finally, I have to thank my patient and punctilious editor, Ed Buscombe, for his encouragement and for his careful reading of this manuscript. Film credits were compiled by Markku Salmi. Illustrations are from the Stills, Posters and Design Department of the British Film Institute. The picture on p. 33 is courtesy of the Academy of Motion Picture Arts and Sciences.

Out of the sunshine and into the shadows

1

> It has all the characteristics of the classic forties film as I respond to it. It's in black and white, it has fast badinage, it's very witty, a story from the classic age. It has Edward G. Robinson, and Barbara Stanwyck and Fred MacMurray and the tough voice-over. It has brilliantly written dialogue, and the perfect score by Miklos Rosza. It's Billy Wilder's best movie ... practically anybody's best movie.
>
> Woody Allen[1]

Agreed. With amendments. Extensive ones. For *Double Indemnity* acts as a kind of purgative, at once bringing out the worst in us while making us feel so much the better for it. As such it contains more devious felicities than memory, however fond, can summon up in the course of a casual conversation. It has, as well, more dark virtues than we may be able to pick up as – warmed, relaxed, our critical faculties disarmed by the nostalgic impulse – we revisit it via home video or late-night television. It is, in fact, a movie that not only withstands rigorous scrutiny, but actually improves the more closely we study it, the more we know about the circumstances of its creation.

All the good qualities Woody Allen quickly enumerated for his biographer, Eric Lax, obviously deserve additional consideration. But there are others he did not mention which must be taken up as well. These, indeed, account for much of the film's powerful initial impact and for its continuing – and still growing – claim on our attention.

Perhaps the most basic of them, made clear only if one happens to read James M. Cain's original tale while studying the film version, is the craftsmanship with which the screenplay is fashioned. The wit which Allen rightly admires is not present in Cain's text. While its prose is admirably straightforward, and aware of the ironies in which it is dealing, you will not find much 'badinage' in it. That's the creation of Wilder and his screenwriting collaborator, Raymond Chandler. Their dialogue is just a little jazzier than any we are likely to hear in life. More important, though, their adaptation shrewdly and smoothly solves problems of structure and characterization that the novelist did not work out very carefully. The gain in plausibility is incalculable. And it is accomplished without blurring the bleakness of Cain's instinctive existentialism.

Imagery is the movie's other great strength – more immediately apparent to most viewers than the subtle remodelings Wilder and Chandler undertook when they moved into this property and made it their own. Allen's glancing reference to the film stock on which the film was shot does not quite cover this matter, as he would surely agree. Wilder is not a director who frames his shots eccentrically or cuts for shock effect. He is fond of saying (with a degree of false modesty) that since he doesn't much like shooting, he does whatever he can to keep the job simple. But he is a man who likes to work in close, not to say claustrophobic, quarters. And he is, even in his comedies, powerfully drawn to what I think of as night-for-day shooting; that is to say, rooms that are quite dimly lit even though we know the sun is shining outside. Chiaroscuro, shadow projections, shafts of bright light entering the frame at arresting angles – these are among Wilder's favorite devices, and *Double Indemnity*, which was his third film as director, represents his first full-scale orchestration of them. It may not be too much to say, indeed, that like the subsequent *Sunset Boulevard* it is a drama about light, about a man lured out of the sunshine and into the shadows.

Be that as it may, it must be said that the movie's visual style analogizes very well with its literary style. It is no more 'realistic' than its dialogue, but it is certainly not expressionistic, either. Perhaps the best way to put it is this: stylistically the film presses firmly against the imagistic conventions of American movies of its time without shattering them by a resort to inflated stylization. Working this borderline it manages simultaneously to reinforce the most potent quality of Cain's work – its air of doomy portent – while adding felt realistic substance to a story that was originally written in some haste for magazine serialization by an author who lacked time, space and perhaps inclination for extended descriptive detail. Put simply, the movie has a very firm sense of place – no movie, documentary or fictional, offers a better sense of how the Los Angeles of its moment looked – but at the same time it energizes that reality with a subtle air of menace. And few movies of any era have more deliciously proved the writerly adage that landscape is character. You could charge L.A. as a co-conspirator in the crimes this movie relates.

The *noir* style

Dialogue and imagery (and, yes, performance – the actors Allen mentions were never better than they are in this film) transform an essentially banal and in some respects unpersuasive narrative. They impart to Cain's story something it also did not have in its rather tatty original form, namely weight and conviction. They, more than the tale they tell, are the source of *Double Indemnity*'s original impact, and they remain the basis of its continuing hold on us. To put the point simply, their singular qualities are the source of the film's singular – no other word will do – authority.

That authority was recognized immediately, even though it was not at all well defined by its first reviewers. A number of them, in fact, were hesitant in their praise, some because they had trouble categorizing the film, others because they were morally offended by it. But whatever judgments they expressed, they still treated *Double Indemnity* with a certain respect, grasping that this was a movie to conjure with, even if they didn't quite know why or how to go about it. The same was true within the industry. The picture did not win any Academy Awards, but it did get seven nominations, recognition few crime films before or since have received. Hollywood didn't quite understand what it had on its hands, either, but it certainly was something – that much it could see. And try somehow to imitate.

Double Indemnity placed its first viewers at a double disadvantage. The most obvious of them was that the genre to which it quite clearly belongs, *film noir*, had not yet been named, let alone anatomized: the first public use of the term appears to have been in a French film journal in 1946, and it did not become common American critical coinage for at least another twenty-five years. There was thus no convenient tradition with which to link *Double Indemnity*, no simple way of defining it through apt comparison. James Agee, for example, evoked *Madame Bovary* and the whole fictional tradition of bourgeois adultery when he reviewed it.[2] Bosley Crowther in the *New York Times* mentioned French realism, without defining what he meant by the term.[3]

The other problem confronting *Double Indemnity*'s contemporary commentators was its source. The film's literary antecedents seemed at the time utterly disreputable, and in those days literary antecedents were everything (or very nearly so) in determining the 'seriousness' of an American movie. It was almost impossible to admit that a major film could be drawn from a source the 'trashiness' of which everyone felt obliged to insist upon when they considered it. Therefore the positive response to the film that instinct generated was often tempered, in 1944, by second thoughts emanating from those centers of the brain which house the Mandarin impulse.

Today, almost a half century later, film and literary scholarship having proceeded apace, these defects in the original response to *Double Indemnity* enhance its historical importance, therefore its air of authority. They show us that in the intervening years we have at least a little expanded the range of our response to certain kinds of movies and writing. Indeed, I would argue that the success of the movie itself, in particular the respectability conferred on it by the several Academy Award nominations it received, played a key role in that expansion, from which (pleasant bit of circularity here) its own reputation has profited.

We know, of course, that despite its lack of a proper French name, the manner we now so easily identify as *film noir* was beginning to take form, critically unremarked, in the early 40s. We also know that genre experts have traced the roots of this style back to the gangster

Above and overleaf:
Film noir's characteristic images

cycle of the 30s and beyond that to the German Expressionism of the 20s (to which Billy Wilder can also trace his roots). But having acknowledged all that, I still think it is plausible to argue that *Double Indemnity*, offering as it did such a bold and artful example of *film noir*'s characteristic images and themes, focused serious attention on that manner as no previous film had done. It can also be argued that the film's success turned a style until then only occasionally resorted to into a full-scale commercial cycle, which then, by the sheer weight of its numbers, turned *film noir* into one of the significant signatures of its historical moment. A simple set of statistics, gathered by Alain Silver and Elizabeth Ward in their indispensable *Film Noir* encyclopedia,[4] supports this point: they list four American *films noirs* for 1941, four for 1942, two for 1943, seven that shared 1944 release with *Double Indemnity*. Thereafter, though, the numbers begin a startling rise: 16 for 1945, 24 for 1946, 29 for 1947, and so on until a tapering off begins in 1952.

Double Indemnity had, I believe, an analogous effect on people's understanding of the literary (or must one still say sub-literary?) tradition it drew on. This is less immediately obvious, and it is more difficult to explain. But it is necessary to consider it.

Begin with the fact that the very phrase *film noir* derives from a literary source. It is a variation on the French term for a certain sort of lowlife novel, the *roman noir*. This, in turn, was related to the trademark phrases, *série noir* and *fleuve noir*, by which Parisian publishers identified the translations and imitations of the American 'tough guy' or 'hard-boiled' mysteries and crime novels they began publishing in series in the late 1930s and early 40s. James M. Cain was among the authors represented in these books. So were such contemporaries as Dashiell Hammett, W. R. Burnett, Horace McCoy, Cornell Woolrich and, latterly, Raymond Chandler. Now observe that the connection between cinematic and literary *noir* was not hard to trace. Many of the *films noirs* that immediately preceded *Double Indemnity* in the early 40s were based on works by these writers (*The Maltese Falcon, High Sierra, The Glass Key, Phantom Lady, Murder, My Sweet*), as were many that immediately followed.

This close connection between a 'school' of writers who had first been identified as such in the late 30s (much to their own distaste, since they mostly disdained one another's work) and the movie style that emerged in the next decade was not, so far as I know, much noticed at the time in the United States. But the 'cinematic' quality of their work had been recognized. And held against them, of course.

The first American critic to write at all seriously about any of these writers was Edmund Wilson, who in 1940 published 'The Boys in the Back Room', a series of essays (later expanded into a short book) about writers who had lived at least for a time in California and used the state as a setting.[5] It was a rather awkward grouping, gathering under the same tent such disparate figures as John O'Hara, John Steinbeck, William Saroyan and, in the book version, Nathanael West. But the first of these pieces was devoted to Cain, McCoy and Eric Knight, author of *Lassie Come Home*, who in a different (not to say schizophrenic) mood, and under a pen name, had written *You Play the Black and the Red Comes Up*, which he may have meant as a parody of tough-guy writing but which reads like the real thing. Though many of them, including Cain, had been highly praised by book page reviewers, this piece constituted the first recognition, however reluctant, the 'hardboiled' writers received from a critic with real standards and credentials, and Cain was grateful enough even for faint praise to write Wilson a friendly, somewhat self-justifying letter after the essay appeared.

The critic observed what others had previously noticed, that Cain's style 'stemmed originally from Hemingway, but it was Hemingway turned picaresque'. He also noted its connections 'with the new school of mystery writers of the type of Dashiell Hammett'. What Wilson had no reason to know, since his mind was fixed elsewhere, was that the Hemingway connection was more apparent than real. Hammett and Hemingway developed their styles at roughly the same time. The dates of Hammett's first detective stories, written very much in the idiom of his later, more famous novels, coincide with the dates of Hemingway's first fiction, they do not follow it. But they appeared in a humble, if now legendary, pulp mystery magazine, *Black Mask* – which, interestingly, had been co-founded by H. L. Mencken and George Jean Nathan as a way of helping to subsidize their more elegant magazine, *The Smart Set* – so it was automatically assumed that Hammett must have been aping one of his betters. It is also assumed that his own influence was small compared to Hemingway's, but that isn't true either.

The little world of pulp fiction writers was much more likely to look to one of their own as a model than they were to someone like Hemingway. That's especially so in this case, for after a couple of changes of ownership *Black Mask* came under the editorship of one Joseph T. ('Cap') Shaw, who liked Hammett's work better than that of any of the other writers he inherited, and urged his other contributors to use it as a model. The greatest of them, Raymond Chandler, credited Hammett as his progenitor, though he later studied Hemingway closely enough to write a parody of his style. Cain, however, was never a *Black Mask* writer, and seems not to have read the magazine. He was like its writers only in this one respect: he insisted that he had read very little Hemingway in the period when he was forming his own style. He instead very plausibly credited Ring Lardner with having a larger influence on him. As we will see, he was also clearly influenced by Mencken, for whose *American Mercury*, a magazine that stressed clean, lithe prose, he wrote extensively.

In short, it would have been closer to the mark not to insist on Hemingway's influence on the others, but to observe that he, like all these writers and many more besides, was shaped by the revolution in journalistic style that began before World War I, continued to develop after it and insisted on a new simplicity of manner and objectivity of outlook in reporting.

Wilson was also determined to find an unflattering connection between the writers he was reviewing and Hollywood. For he was certain that they had been corrupted by their work as screenwriters for an industry with, as he put it, an 'appalling record of talent wasted and depraved'. Again, he had things slightly wrong. Their fiction was produced in their 'off-time' from the studios, he said, implying that their real interest and energies were applied to screenplays. The reverse was actually true. Cain regarded movie work as he had formerly regarded journalism, as a way of supporting more serious literary endeavors. Nor did Wilson know that Cain, like Hammett, had never been happily employed in the movies and never really acquired the knack for writing successful screenplays, though he would have liked to learn since the money was good and he was always in need of it. He was in and out of studio writers' buildings for almost twenty years, enjoying the camaraderie they offered and cashing any number of solid studio paychecks. But in that time he earned only three shared screen credits, for he found that his employment opportunities were limited by his inability to write easily to order and that they correlated rather closely with the rise and fall of his literary repute. If he had a hot book or story in the market-place, his phone rang; if things were quiet for him in the literary world they tended to be quiet for him in Hollywood too. In other words, he was perfectly willing to be 'depraved' by his day job, but found certain practical difficulties hindered that process.

Given his tastes, and the moral fervor he brought to the literary enterprise, and expected of others, it is neither surprising nor discreditable that Wilson rather missed the point about Cain and the other writers of his type. The critic never really understood the practical attitude of working writers, willing to turn their hands to almost any kind of assignment if it was reasonably respectable and reasonably well-paid. It is not that they aspired to and failed to attain the standards of high literature. Most of them aspired instead to 'professionalism' (a word they often used), the ability to make a decent job of work out of anything they turned their hands to – which often included 'serious' literature. Nor is it true that many of them 'sold out'; most of them made very little money and were as oppressed by its lack as any poet, or for that matter Edmund Wilson, whose letters are full of economic woe. The 'boys in the back room' were, in their way, responding to the same social and psychological issues that the folks in the more brightly lit salon up-front were. They were processing the same data, as it were, but in a different way, with considerably more modest ambitions yet with no less seriousness. This is particularly true of the table to which Cain's chair was drawn up, for the pervasive sin of all popular writing – including much movie writing – which is falsifying sentimentality, was not one in which they trafficked.

Still, it is very much to Wilson's credit that, dubious as he was about this kind of popular fiction, he did find value in it (he would later write enthusiastically about Raymond Chandler). Cain and his fellows were, he wrote, 'the poets of the tabloid murder', and he recognized that this was an aspect of American reality that both high and low culture were missing. He apparently didn't think the former could do much with it (though he mentioned Dreiser's *An American Tragedy* approvingly), but the latter could. In his essay's most arresting passage he called Cain's novels 'a kind of devil's parody of the movies', and went on to lament the fact that, to date, the movies had not been able to avail themselves of his spirit. 'All the things that have been excluded by the Catholic censorship: sex, debauchery, unpunished crime, sacrilege against the church – Mr Cain has let them loose in these stories with a gusto as of pent-up ferocity that the reader cannot but share. What a pity that it is impossible for such a writer to create and produce his own pictures!'

All right, there was patronization in that judgment. And wrong-headedness too, because it was not disgust with movie censorship that moved Cain to write as he did. But there were the beginnings of truth in Wilson's observation. The movie industry's acquiescence in censorship was a function of its lust for middle-class respectability, which it had more or less achieved by the mid-1940s, when its super-patriotic war work had brought it into close, mutually admiring relationship with Washington. What it needed now, especially in its melodramas, was an enlivening dose of the down and dirty – a note of 'devilishness'.

Wilson must naturally be forgiven for not seeing in 1940 that the delay in bringing Cain's work to the screen – it was a slight liberalization, later in the decade, of their interpretation of the Production Code by the Motion Picture Association's censors that permitted Wilder and Paramount to begin contemplating *Double Indemnity* – worked to his advantage, and the medium's as well. For it was in that interim that, as we have seen, the *noir* style began to develop. Wilder's genius was to see – how consciously it is impossible to say – that this baroque manner would be aesthetically redeeming for Cain's disturbing matter, giving it a richness, a resonance, even, if you will, a touch of class that the writer's blunt exploration of brutal emotions by means of simple declarative sentences had not had on the printed page.

Wilder could, by resort to this manner, disarm (or at least distract) those who would otherwise have found this story impossibly sordid and cynical. Best of all, he could acknowledge what movies had until then hesitated to admit openly, the anti-romantic possibility that sexual attraction can easily turn into sexual obsession, and that once it does it has a terrible power to victimize and criminalize. This, of course, would turn out to be one of *film noir*'s great themes and, in a less obvious way, one of Wilder's great themes too.

Finally, just because of the muscular weight his film added to material that many had found underdeveloped, powered mainly by a kind of feverishness, Wilder made it impossible for subsequent critics to deal with Cain and his school as dismissively as Wilson had. This move, and the genre that its success encouraged, had to be reckoned with. And that meant that its literary sources had to be reckoned with too. For better or worse, a scholarly industry, including incomprehensible structural analyses of Cain's work and the movies derived from it, was one of *Double Indemnity*'s unintended consequences. For better or worse, we are now required to take Jim Thompson – and Elmore Leonard – more seriously than we probably should in part because of the train of events Wilder set in motion in 1943. And that says nothing about enduring the *film noir* pastiches a couple of generations of impressionable film school graduates insist on turning out for us now. But the price is relatively small. And the gains both in the expressive range available to the movies and in the range of responses to them which are now available to the serious audience are substantial.

2

Billy Wilder recently remarked that he had done a number of movies because he wanted to try something in a manner he admired. *Love in the Afternoon*, for example, was his homage to Lubitsch, *Witness for the Prosecution* his tribute to Hitchcock. And *Double Indemnity*? Why, he said, that was his testimonial to *The Postman Always Rings Twice*.

Very appropriate, for a number of reasons. Not the least of which is that *Double Indemnity* was created by James M. Cain in full knowledge that he was doing his own homage to *Postman*, his wildly successful first novel. Maybe he was not quite practising self-plagiarism, but certainly there was – in the eight-part serial he sold to *Liberty* magazine for $5,000 for publication in 1936 – more than a mere echo of his previous work. Both tell essentially the same story: an all too compliant male is enthralled by a strong and scheming woman. With her motivating it and with him taking care of the details, the adulterous couple execute a perfect murder of the woman's husband. Then, when they are virtually in the clear, fate (or irony) swipes them with its big blundering paw and they receive their just desserts – but for the wrong reasons.

Stylistically, too, the works are similar. Both are novella-length, both are told in staccato style: short sentences, short paragraphs, bold swatches of dialogue, quick, punchy descriptions of action. There is nothing in them that hinders narrative efficiency. In that sense they are like mystery novels, though with the puzzle left out, of course. We know from the beginning whodunit, because we are there with the murderers, planning their crimes all the way – or to use *Double Indemnity*'s catchphrase, 'straight down the line'. The other literary form these works resemble is the movie treatment – pellmell, but very logical in its statement of a narrative line.

There are, to be sure, some differences between the two books. For example, an insurance policy and an insurance claims investigator, respectively a comparatively minor matter and minor figure in the novel, are central in the serial – the former the prime motive for murder, the latter a crucial figure in working out the narrative. Cain had talked to insurance people while plotting *Postman*, and recalled that after it came out some of them had urged him to look for more ideas involving insurance cases. They pointed out that with company money at stake, insurance claims investigators were often more implacable than the police in pursuing suspicious deaths.

Perhaps more important, *Postman* is more explicitly erotic than *Double Indemnity*. The sex scenes in the former have a brutal, vivid, animalistic haste about them; the sex scenes in the latter end after a few mild kisses, doubtless because Cain was writing for the family magazine market, no more daring in these matters than Hollywood was at the time. This was a defect, incidentally, that Wilder and Chandler, still operating after all under Production Code rules, never quite compensated for in their adaptation.

But the resemblances between the two works are more significant, or at least more interesting, than their contrasts. In any case, what needs to be stressed at the moment is that Hollywood, no less than Edmund Wilson, could see that these stories were born to be filmed. *Postman* was critically acclaimed, a best-seller and – the best

Lana Turner and John Garfield in *The Postman Always Rings Twice* (1946)

thing that could happen to a novel in those days – banned in Boston. When *Double Indemnity* began running in *Liberty*, rumor had it that it increased the magazine's circulation by eight million copies. This is doubtless an exaggeration, but unquestionably it enhanced *Liberty*'s newsstand sales perceptibly.

In any event, the clamor over *Postman* was so great that at least two studios, MGM and Columbia, were willing to take a chance that they could 'lick the story' (as the saying went), despite their certainty that the Motion Picture Producers Association censors, the Breen office, would look askance at the enterprise. Columbia, indeed, dropped out of the bidding for the story when the censors warned studios that they were unlikely to approve any adaptation of *Postman*, no matter how it was scrubbed up. MGM decided to go ahead anyway; as the biggest lion in the Hollywood jungle its desires carried more weight with Breen than little Columbia did. But Breen's opposition did cut in half the $50,000 price Cain's agent originally thought he could get for the property. It was not until Wilder's film succeeded, and twelve years had passed, that MGM, having commissioned several scripts that failed to retain the values of the story they bought while satisfying the censors' objections, finally made the picture in a rather cold, sanitized (and miscast) version. That studio, always more committed to gloss than grit, never did get the knack of *noir*.

Cain suffered the same sort of financial punishment when *Double Indemnity* was placed on the Hollywood market. Before the serial began appearing in *Liberty*, Cain's agent showed mimeographed copies of the piece to the studios and reported to the author that he had never seen such interest in an unpublished short work. Conversations with story executives led him to believe he could get $25,000 for it. Then, when the serial began to appear, the Breen office declared that under no circumstances could it be brought to the screen, and all talk stilled. When *Double Indemnity* was finally sold to Paramount, almost a decade later, the best price Cain's new agent, the highly regarded H. N. Swanson, could get for it was $15,000. In all, the Breen office had cost the author $35,000.

In an odd way, the censorious opposition to Cain's works enhanced their value to others, if not to Cain. They became, to appropriate the old publicity line, 'the pictures they said could never be made', tempting and challenging Hollywood. If someone could finally end the frustration by accomplishing the nice trick of bringing one of them to the screen still steaming but with Breen office opposition cooled, he would obviously become a figure to be reckoned with.

Enter Billy Wilder. Born in Vienna, educated in the ways of the world as a journalist and screenwriter in Berlin during the years of the Weimar Republic, he was among the first Jews to flee Hitler's Germany for Hollywood, arriving after a brief stay in Paris where he co-directed his first film, an experience so unpleasant for him that he vowed never to repeat it. He enjoyed no great success as a screenwriter in America until Paramount teamed him with Charles Brackett, who was everything Wilder was not. Silver-haired, seemly in manner, Harvard-educated, the scion of an old and excellent Republican family from upstate New York, Brackett was a sometime journalist and novelist who would in the late 1940s become president of the Academy of Motion Picture Arts and Sciences.

They were an odd couple, and they fought their way through some fourteen years of collaboration. But somehow – even when they were not speaking to each other, or when Brackett was throwing things at Wilder who was, in his own account, ducking and catching them – they wrote some of the most charming films of the pre-war years. Beginning with Lubitsch's *Bluebeard's Eighth Wife*, among other great titles of the great age of romantic comedy they wrote *Midnight, Ninotchka* and *Ball of Fire*. But Wilder came to feel that their subsequent work on *Arise My Love* and *Hold Back the Dawn* – more serious films that still had a rather continental air about them – was desecrated, mostly by director Mitchell Leisen (whose tamperings with Preston Sturges's writing had also motivated Sturges to turn to directing). To protect their work he proposed that in future Brackett should produce their scripts which he, Wilder, would direct. By 1943 they had done two films in this manner – *The Major and the Minor*, a very curious comedy in which a 32-year-old Ginger Rogers pretends to be a girl less than half her age (so that she can take a train home on a child's half-fare), and a sharply realized espionage story, *Five Graves to Cairo*, particularly memorable for Erich von Stroheim's deliciously epicene portrayal of General Rommel.

Both pictures were well-made and well-received. They

established Wilder as an intelligent, reliable director. But they did not – could not in their nature – 'set Hollywood back on its heels', as Wilder told an interviewer in 1944 he wanted to do, as he doubtless knew he had to do if he was ever to separate himself from the rest of the pack. He began contemplating a musical, at least in part because, coming from him, with his reputation for the sardonic and the sophisticated, it would represent a change of pace people would talk about.

Others had already started to work the kind of variants on that genre's formula that Wilder wanted to try. In the 1944 interview he cited the success of *Cover Girl* as one of the factors that dissuaded him. But Arthur Freed's so-called 'unit' at MGM was also beginning to function, making musicals quite different in spirit and sophistication from most of those that had preceded them (in 1944 it would make *Meet Me in St. Louis*, as big a turning-point for screen musicals as *Oklahoma!*, produced a year earlier, had been for stage musicals). No, a musical was not the answer for Wilder.

At which point *Double Indemnity* came to Wilder's attention. There is some dispute as to how it did so. Despite Cain's original belief that it should not be published in book form, he was persuaded to include it with two other pieces of magazine fiction in *Three of a Kind*, which Knopf (a firm that published almost all the important *noir* writers, among them Hammett, Burnett and Chandler) brought out in 1943. Cain's agent Swanson circulated proofs of the book to the studios, and as Cain would later tell the story to his biographer, Roy Hoopes, Wilder enquired one day about the absence of his secretary and was told that she was 'still in the ladies' room reading "that story".' 'What story?' 'Some story Mr Swanson left here.' Soon the secretary reappeared, carrying the *Three of a Kind* proofs, which Wilder took home with him that night to read.[6]

Wilder's recollection is different. He remembers that *Double Indemnity*, like the *Saturday Evening Post* story on which *The Major and the Minor* was based, was brought to his attention by Joseph Sistrom, a bright young staff producer who bore an uncanny resemblance to Rudyard Kipling and had actually played the writer in *Gunga Din*. To this day Wilder insists that Sistrom deserves more credit than he has been accorded by history or the credits of *Double Indemnity* (where he is listed only as 'Associate Producer'). Sistrom always had three things in his hands, Wilder recalled: 'a cigarette, a bottle of beer and a greasy soft-covered book'. He also recalled that *Double Indemnity* was presented to him in the form of stapled together, falling apart pages from *Liberty*, now seven years old.

Whatever the case, this was an idea whose time had come. Wilder admired *Postman*, knew *Double Indemnity* by reputation, and, for that matter, knew Cain. The novelist had been under contract at Columbia when Wilder got his first Hollywood job at the studio. Discovering Wilder, extremely anxious to make good, pounding away at his typewriter at 10 a.m. one morning, Cain advised him that Columbia writers usually didn't get going until around 11:45, in time for studio boss Harry Cohn's customary late arrival, when he expected to hear their machines busily arattle.

But neither acquaintance with Cain nor regard for his famous first novel nor yet the obvious advantage in becoming the first film-maker to bring one of his forbidden works to the screen can entirely account for Wilder's immediate enthusiasm for this project. Wilder said recently that he was drawn to the book because it was about 'my kind of people'. And what kind of people are they? 'My kind of people are people who do photographable things,' he said simply.

Heaven knows, that's true of *Double Indemnity*'s principals. But there is more to Wilder's enthusiasm for the book than that. He had, I think, a special emotional affinity for Cain's work based on the fact that they arrived in that strange new country, Southern California, at around the same time and were bemused, if not startled, by a landscape and an atmosphere entirely unlike anything either of them had ever known. They were both also, perhaps, liberated artistically by its sense of newness, rawness, its lack of traditional social and cultural constraints.

That is particularly obvious in the novelist's case. The son of the president of a small Maryland college, he worked on an army newspaper during World War One, and joined the Baltimore *Sun* after his discharge from the service. It was there that he first came to know H. L. Mencken, the paper's great ornament, and he used material he had gathered on assignment for the *Sun* for his first major magazine piece, about a West Virginia coalminers' strike, which he published in *The Atlantic*. After leaving the paper he wrote his first *American Mercury* articles for Mencken, continuing that association after he went to work for Walter Lippmann, the most famous (not to say intimidating) American intellectual-journalist of his day, perhaps of this century, who in the 1920s edited the editorial pages of what was then generally regarded as the most literate of American newspapers, the New York *World*. Cain joined its staff in 1924, writing hundreds of short, light, anonymous editorials for Lippmann – mostly graceful little familiar essays about the passing scene – in the process becoming friends with another famous journalist, Arthur Krock, later to be head of the New York *Times* Washington bureau and a pundit second only to Lippmann in his influence on serious readers. These two rather grand figures remained Cain's friends, Lippmann rather improbably serving as informal agent for *Postman* and Krock, equally curiously, supplying a jacket blurb for it, as well as the inspiration for one of *Double Indemnity*'s major plot points.

Mencken remained an equally important mentor, for Cain's bylines in the *Mercury*, undoubtedly the most influential literary-political journal of the 1920s, gave him the beginnings of a public reputation and he continued to write for it even after moving to Los Angeles. When the *World* folded in 1931, Cain joined the *New Yorker*, serving briefly as one of its many managing editors, or 'Jesuses' as they were known around the office. (The magazine's founder, Harold Ross, always believed initially that each of them would bring order out of the chaotic publication process that marked the magazine's early years, then played Judas to them when they proved unequal to the task.)

This background indicates that Cain was very far from the studio hack Edmund Wilson apparently imagined him to be. Or perhaps knowing something of it made the critic testy about what would have seemed to him a fall from the true literary faith. Be that as it may, this busy career masks a frustration. For throughout this period Cain entertained hopes for himself as a novelist, though he never completed a long work of fiction that satisfied him. He did, however, write a series of imaginary, if observationally well-grounded, 'dialogues' which satirized a variety of typical American public figures. These he published in the *Mercury*, and then gathered into a little book which Alfred A. Knopf, Mencken's close friend and publisher, spotting what he believed to be a novelist *manqué*, brought out under the title *Our Government*. His contract with Cain contained an option on two more books, which the publisher hoped would be fiction.

The form of his *Our Government* pieces made Cain saleable in Hollywood and, tiring of the *New Yorker*'s messy ways, which left him little energy to write, he asked his agent one day in 1931 to see what he could do for him in Hollywood. By the end of the afternoon the man had an offer from Paramount. In a matter of weeks Cain was on the lot on Melrose Avenue; in a matter of months, he was off it, beginning a seventeen-year odyssey in and out of virtually every studio gate in town.

Curious that a man with the gift for brisk melodramatic plotting and the talent for dialogue he would soon demonstrate in his first published novel never mastered the screenwriting trade. That may be because screenplays are not written in the first person, and it was apparently the belated discovery, while working on a short story, that first-person narration somehow freed him creatively, that enabled Cain to pursue *Postman* to its successful end. It may also be that he was frustrated by the fact that most screenplays did not explore those aspects of American life – the dour and dirty – which fascinated him. Nor was Hollywood at this time greatly interested in the curious variants on the American lifestyle that were beginning to take shape in Southern California, its own backyard.

The most important of these was, to use a now familiar term anachronistically, its car culture (which features in the death plots of both *Postman* and *Double Indemnity*). As a man who had grown up in the more confined and heavily populated Maryland landscape and had passed much of his adult life pressed within Manhattan's tight grid, he responded enthusiastically to the open roads of his new environment. The quality that had originally recommended Los Angeles to movie-makers, its ready access to a rich variety of landscapes – desert, mountains, shore, farmland, even a foreign country (Mexico) – while providing at least a plausible, photographable sketch of the metropolis that was soon to arise, spoke vividly to Cain as well. He was always buzzing about in and around the city, up and down the coast, just like the characters in his books.

Gas stations and roadside restaurants, wayside enterprises of all kinds, fascinated him. The signs their proprietors set up along the highways bespoke small hopes and pinched dreams, which, modest as they were, often enough ended in foreclosure. The exotic local architecture was also a kind of dreamwork, gaudy, insubstantial, carelessly aspiring, and mostly without organic roots in this countryside. The bland local cuisine, which preoccupied much of 'Paradise', the long essay on California that Cain contributed to the *Mercury* in 1933, perhaps supported his developing notions about this curious culture. It takes time, a certain rootedness in tradition, to cook well, and restless Southern Californians, constantly on the move but actually going nowhere, didn't make that sort of commitment to this or any other cultural enterprise that required a long attention span. They invented drive-ins instead.

Cain even noted, in his essay, that the characteristic local crime consisted of a mysterious disappearance and then the discovery some time later of a body disposed of in the wild, open country that so closely abutted, even interpenetrated, the city. This type of crime remains a feature of Los Angeles life even now, after the cuisine has achieved near-comic preciocity, the symphony orchestra is world-class, the major newspaper first-rate; and it continues to suggest what it did to Cain – a population of strangers drifting about, surrendering to heedless impulse. *The Postman Always Rings Twice, Double Indemnity, Mildred Pierce* all depend to some degree on this sense of place, and its effect on character. Nor does one wonder in the slightest that Albert Camus cited *Postman* as the inspiration for *L'Etranger*.

If Cain, an American after all, was stirred – and unblocked – by the discovery of what was almost an alien culture developing within his native land, how much more stirring and how much more alien, even surreal, that culture must have seemed to a European like Wilder. Indeed his *Postman*, that is to say the Wilder movie that reflects his alien's vision of the restlessness and pathos of roadside America, is his great, relentlessly cynical, almost unbearably cold *Ace in the Hole* (retitled, after dismal initial grosses, *The Big Carnival*) of 1951.

The largest difference between novelist and director lay, of course, in the nature of their responses to lowlife American culture. Some of that difference can be traced to their contrasting sense of the American language. Cain, coming out of the Mencken tradition, with its stress on straightforward exposition, wrote a clean, muscular prose; and his dialogue, very much admired by critics, readers and the movie producers who wanted to hear it on the screen, caught the rhythms of ordinary American speech very accurately – or at least created that illusion persuasively.

Wilder, like other immigrants (Vladimir Nabokov comes to mind in this respect), heard something wild and strange in American speech. What sounded like clichés to the native-born sounded like fresh metaphors to a wry spirit listening closely. It is no accident that one of the best early Wilder-Brackett comedies, *Ball of Fire*, is about a nightclub singer (played by Barbara Stanwyck, it is perhaps significant to observe), in trouble with mobsters, who takes refuge in a think tank – where the professors are studying the American language, with special emphasis on the vernacular.

There was, as well, what we might term a philosophical difference between Cain and Wilder. Many of the director's movies concern some outrageous scam or impersonation, and as Stephen Farber has pointed out, some part of Wilder admires the creative imagination and energy that goes into these activities.[7] A man who had to hustle hard for a living in his early Berlin days, and in his early Hollywood days too, perhaps cannot help but find the con (and con-men and women) irresistible. That was not true of Cain. *Double Indemnity* is the only one of his *romans noirs* that revolves round a dirty trick, and his attitude carried no secret admiration for it, as the cheekier Wilder's does.

In the restlessness and fecklessness of Southern California life, Cain saw a place where the hype and shuck were more likely to occur than they were in more stable societies. Here he found a fateful, even tragic aura: at the far end of the continent, the far end of the American dream – something like that, anyway. For Wilder, however, this was not just the end of a continent, it was the ends of the earth, about as far away as he could get from his native Vienna and from the Berlin of the 1920s where his mature sensibility was formed. Both cities had taught him to recognize decadence when he saw it. And both had taught him that the appropriate response to it was sardonic laughter.

As of 1943, after a decade spent absorbing the strangeness of his exotic new environment, a decade in which the majority of the films he co-wrote had invoked the romantic spirit of a Europe that no longer existed (and had existed, anyway, mainly as a film and theatrical convention), Wilder was ready, at last, to turn his attention to the new world. Or perhaps one should say *his* new world, which Cain had concretized for him in a form that admirably suited the needs of his career at this juncture.

3

This was not a venture in which staid Charlie Brackett was inclined to join his collaborator. His judgment on *Double Indemnity* was 'Disgusting'. Wilder then proposed that Cain himself be brought in to work with him on the adaptation, but he was at that moment under contract at Fox. Sistrom, the resident expert on popular fiction, then suggested Raymond Chandler, just winding down from that great four-year outburst of creativity (1939–43) in which, at the rate of one a year, he had produced his first and by common consent best novels. Wilder had not read these books, but when he did he was much taken by them. He recently remembered two lines from them: 'There's nothing as empty as an empty swimming pool', and a description of an old man's thinning hair, clinging to his scalp 'like wild flowers fighting for life on a bare rock', and added, 'Anyone who can write like that is all right with me.' To put the point simply, Chandler wrote in pictures – his books are full of vivid, occasionally strained, metaphorical descriptions of people, places and things. This was, if you will, cinematic writing of a different kind from Cain's, but complementary to it, obviously.

Chandler's dialogue had its own kind of toughness and speed, funnier than Cain's, more baroque, but in its briskness not entirely dissimilar from it. His expositional prose, however, was much richer and, perhaps most important, he had, as everyone knows, an unsurpassed gift for evoking the spirit, the atmosphere, of the Los Angeles of his day. This was the realm in which his talent was unquestionably much larger than Cain's.

He, too, viewed California with an alien's eyes. Nebraska-born, Chandler had been educated at an English Public School and had served in the Canadian army in World War One, and though he came to California much earlier than either Wilder or Cain (he was there briefly before the war, and returned immediately after it, working for many years as an executive with various oil companies), there was more than a little of the fastidious displaced Anglophile in his point of view – one slightly disappointed to discover there were places on earth that would never be a little corner of England.

To put all this simply, Raymond Chandler was, on paper, perfect casting for this particular screenwriting job. In person, however, he presented a more difficult case. He was 55 when he reported to Paramount to discuss the assignment with Wilder and Sistrom, a loner and an alcoholic, set in his habits, in his low opinions of screenwriting and, as it happened, of James M. Cain. Indeed, not long before he had written to his publisher that he was tired of being coupled with Hammett and Cain by the reviewers. The former he thought just 'all right'. There were, he wrote, 'a lot of things he could not do, but what he did he did superbly.' Cain, though, was quite a different matter. 'Faugh. Everything he touches smells like a billygoat. He is every kind

Raymond Chandler and Billy Wilder

of writer I detest, a faux naif, a Proust in overalls [!], a dirty little boy with a piece of chalk and a board fence and nobody looking. Such people are the offal of literature, not because they write about dirty things, but because they do it in a dirty way. Nothing hard and clean and ventilated. A brothel with a smell of cheap scent in the front parlor and a bucket of slops at the back door. Do I, for God's sake, sound like that?'[8]

Well, no, of course not. But then neither did Cain. Indeed, to the modern reader the prodigies of moral outrage he occasioned in his first decade as a novelist are quite astonishing. His view of human nature and motives may be grim but his language is chaste, his writing about sex is discreet, and he does not linger long or lovingly over acts of violence. Moreover, in his books transgressors are always in some way punished for their sins. Hard to see why Chandler took him so harshly to task on these matters. Hard to see why so many others did. It is perhaps because he never expressed overt disapproval of the people he wrote about, never sociologized them or drew political morals from their behavior. Perhaps his problem lay in his refusal or inability to imagine a figure like Chandler's immortal private eye, Philip Marlowe, who was tough and knowing, but in his way gallant, and always incorruptible. In Chandler's detective fiction, he was more than a protagonist; he functioned as a center of conventional morality in an otherwise frowsy universe. Indeed, as Chandler makes clear, he suffers poverty, loneliness, a constant sense of his own otherness, precisely because of his rectitude. It may be that some of Cain's continuing appeal derives from his hard-eyed reluctance to insert such a figure into his low-life milieu. In any case, as we shall see, it is the creation of just such a character that makes the Wilder–Chandler adaptation of *Double Indemnity* work better, dramatically speaking, than its source.

That, however, was in the future. For the moment Chandler was simply glad to get a job. At the end of his first meeting with Wilder and Sistrom he agreed to have a go at the script. Then, however, he drew himself up tall, and declared (in Wilder's recollection): 'Gentlemen, I have no agent, but I'm not cheap. I'll tell you right now that this screenplay is going to cost you $750, and you can't have it until a week from Friday.' There spoke a man used to the penny per word payments of the pulps and the paltry advances of Alfred A. Knopf. He left behind, of course, two astonished auditors. But they awaited his return with great interest.

Chandler was not quite as good as his word. He had completed only about sixty-five pages of his screenplay before his next appointment with Wilder and Sistrom, and the director did not think much of it. Mostly, he recalls, Chandler had typed up Cain's dialogue in the best imitation he could manage of screenplay form, adding camera directions and the like. He had not, however, attacked what Wilder judged to be the largest problems presented by the project. 'I don't want technique,' Wilder told the writer, meaning scripted notations of how shots should look, 'that's what I'm for.' Believing Cain's original had not been 'thought out properly', what Wilder wanted chiefly was a collaborator who would help him shore up its shaky underpinnings. 'A screenplay,' as Wilder recently put it, 'is a mixture of poetry and architecture. If you don't have the architecture the fucker will collapse on you.'

Still, Wilder thought he could work with Chandler, who agreed with him about *Double Indemnity*'s structural weakness. He also believed along with Wilder that dialogue would be the least of their problems in making this adaptation. And he agreed to Wilder's plan of attack: a true collaboration from 9:30 to 5:00 every day, working 'every line together'. These terms set, Wilder and Sistrom said there would have to be an adjustment in the pay scale Chandler had demanded. They thought $1000 would be more like it. A $1000 a week, that is.

Or so Wilder recalls. Frank MacShane, Chandler's biographer, reports that Sistrom put in a call to H. N. Swanson, and got him to negotiate the writer's contract with the studio, and that it was only for $750 a week for thirteen weeks – still more money than Chandler had ever made writing.

He earned it. For he and Wilder were essentially antithetical spirits. A picture of the collaborators shows a small, sharp-faced, casually dressed Wilder, looking energetic and eager. He is dwarfed by the older, tweedy, ponderous-seeming Chandler, who was, we know, a shy and solitary man, in contrast to the gregarious Wilder. In time, Chandler came to enjoy the camaraderie of life on the lot. He took pleasure in the company of the writers' table in the commissary, and he even pursued secretaries in the time-honored Hollywood tradition. But cloistered in Wilder's tiny, spartan office, he was not entirely happy.

Wilder was a pacer, often waving the malacca cane he affected in those days under Chandler's nose to emphasize a point. He interrupted their deliberations to take phone calls. At lunch, he enjoyed a drink or two at Lucey's, the favored hangout across the street from the studio. When the atmosphere in his office grew claustrophobic he was apt to suddenly absent himself in the men's room – more often, in Chandler's judgment, than the calls of nature dictated. In short, he drove the older man crazy.

One day, Chandler did not appear for work. Instead, he delivered to Sistrom an ultimatum scribbled on a yellow legal pad. It was a list of Wilder's offences against decorum, and the novelist demanded that the director forswear all of them, including peremptory demands, unaccompanied by the word 'please', that Chandler close an open door or adjust the Venetian blinds when the sun struck the director in the eyes.

Years later, Wilder would analyse Chandler's crotchety response to him. He observed that the writer was an alcoholic trying to stay sober (though Wilder swears he carried a pint bottle in his briefcase, nipping at it when Wilder was in the bathroom). This accounted for his resentment of the director's lunchtime martinis, which in no way affected his blithe functioning. Then, too, many of Wilder's phone calls involved his active and jolly romantic life, and they were upsetting to Chandler, because he was married to a woman some twenty years older than he was, with whom he no longer had a sexual life. He was, in short, 'a disgruntled man', as Wilder put it and, perhaps worse in the eyes of the congenitally puckish director, 'a hard man to get a smile out of'.

Still, Wilder yielded to Chandler's ultimatum. And he has never offered anything but unstinting praise for the novelist's work on their screenplay. Chandler himself offered grudging acknowledgment of the educational benefits he derived from the experience. It was, he said, 'an agonizing experience, and has probably shortened my life; but I learned from it as much about screen writing as I am capable of learning, which is not much.'

It turned out that the famous Cain dialogue, which both men had assumed could be translated to the screen virtually intact was unusable

– 'unspeakable', to use Wilder's word, which he meant literally, not pejoratively. They brought in actors to try to read it, and it fell flat. They brought in Cain himself to see if he could help them analyse the difficulty. At this meeting Sistrom made an observation that remained with Cain. 'All characters in B pictures are too smart,' he said. Meaning, as Cain put it, that 'when a character is too smart, convenient to the author's purpose, everything begins getting awfully slack in the story, and slick.'[9] The people of *Double Indemnity* are not smart; they only think they are.

Out of that meeting came an extraordinarily interesting exchange between the two novelists. Chandler, despite his disapproval of Cain's work, wrote very politely to him about his dialogue:

> Nothing could be more natural and easy and to the point on paper, and yet it doesn't quite play. ... It has a remote effect that I was at a loss to understand. It came to me then that the effect of your written dialogue is partly sound and sense. The rest of the effect is the appearance on the page. Those unevenly shaped hulks of quick-moving speech [one of Cain's innovations was to dispense with the he said/she said identifications at the end of each line in his dialogue exchanges] hit the eye with a sort of explosive effect. You read the stuff in batches, not in individual speech and counterspeech. On the screen, this is all lost, and the essential mildness of the phrasing shows up as lacking in sharpness. They tell me that is the difference between photographable dialogue and written dialogue. For the screen everything has to be sharpened and pointed and wherever possible eluded. But of course you know far more about that than I do.

Cain replied in the same collegial vein.

> I use a completely different system in picture work when I dictate for the ear and pay almost no attention to how it appears to the eye. I have secretly been amused at picture producers who tell me: 'And don't forget to give me plenty of that fast Cain dialogue.' The truth is that Cain dialogue wouldn't play at all, but I think it advisable not to tell them.

He added, significantly: 'Your description of the vague, cloudy way the dialogue sounded when you had it tried with actors is wholly interesting, for in *Double Indemnity* I was trying to capture some of those billowing unrealities you get in a fever dream, and if the dialogue sounded as you say it did, quite possibly I succeeded.'[10]

There is certainly nothing billowy about the film's writing. It is, indeed, 'sharpened and pointed' in a very delicate but also very funny way. Take a very simple thing, the name changes Wilder and Chandler imposed on Cain's central figures. In the film the compliant insurance salesman, Walter Huff, becomes Walter Neff, his inamorata Phyllis Nirdlinger becomes Phyllis Dietrichson. The comical echo set up by their original names is silenced, replaced by names with a harder edge to them.

Or consider the advantages of framing Walter Neff's confession, which proceeds as voice-over narration, within a flashback. This permits the movie to open with a sequence that brilliantly establishes its mood and, indeed, subtly prefigures everything that follows. We see a night street, men working on the pavement in front of an office building; a car careers down a hill toward them, narrowly avoiding

'We see the car run the light'

collision with a truck; the camera cranes up so that a stoplight is to the left of the frame; it changes from 'Go' to 'Stop' and we see the car run the light. This is, of course, a metaphor for everything we are about to learn about the car's occupant, Walter Neff, who has run all the stoplights in his relationship with Phyllis Dietrichson. (That car, by the way, is perfectly cast, for it is a jaunty little coupé, sporty and insubstantial, like Neff himself.) The rest of this opening sequence is equally fine, for Neff staggering to the elevator and then lurching toward his office is seen from the back, in shadow. We don't know for certain that he is the film's star, Fred MacMurray, until he is settled at his desk, lamp and dictaphone switched on, cigarette lit, his confession begun. There is irony in the form this takes – the quotidian interoffice memo, addressed to a man we will soon know better, Barton Keyes, chief claims investigator for The Pacific All-Risk Insurance Company (also a happy renaming, since Neff is an All-Risk sort of guy, not at all a man one would associate with General Fidelity, his company's name in Cain's original story).

This is all wonderful screenwriting (and direction too, of course), setting up the film's mood and premises dramatically, suspensefully,

'His confession begun'

efficiently. Above all, it tells you what you always want to know as a movie starts out – that you are in good hands, the hands of people who know what they're doing and where they're going.

The voice-over is more wry and weary than the first-person narration of the novel, much closer to the voice Chandler's Philip Marlowe used to recount his tales than it is to Cain's flatter tones. For example, Neff describes himself thus: 'Insurance salesman, 35 years old, unmarried, no visible scars until a while ago.'

But it is in the first flashback that the truly significant deviations from the original text begin. In the novel, after a maid has announced Walter, Phyllis, clad in lounging pyjamas, simply enters to tell him that her husband, whom he wishes to see about renewing his automobile insurance, isn't home. In the film, as Walter is in the process of forcing his way past the maid, Phyllis appears at the top of the stairs, wearing nothing but a towel. Quickly describing his errand, Walter eyes her up and down and says: 'I'd hate to think of you getting a scratched fender when you're not . . . covered.' 'I know what you mean,' she replies. 'I've been sunbathing.' 'Hope there weren't any pigeons around,' he says slyly.

Our first sight of Phyllis . . .

And so it goes. She asks him to wait while she dresses. When she reappears the camera is close-up on her lower legs as she comes down the stairs, still buttoning her dress. The shot introduces the ankle bracelet – such a nice touch, signifying lower middle-class commonness, just the sort of adornment a former nurse who has married upward might favor – about which Walter is soon complimenting her. In the book it is freckles across her nose – quite a different resonance – which first arouse his erotic interest.

As in the novel, the subject of accident insurance for Phyllis's husband arises almost immediately, but the terms of the discussion – and Walter's sense that her interest in the subject is not exactly altruistic – are made clearer sooner. Their erotic sparring also begins in this first encounter, another change from the book. Indeed, this sequence contains the exchange that rivets one's commitment to the movie. She has invited him to return the next night, when her husband will be home and available to discuss insurance. Walter, testing the truth of the innuendoes they have been trading, expresses a certain lack of interest in meeting him. 'There's a speed limit in this state – 45 miles per hour,' she snaps.

. . . and the ankle bracelet

> 'How fast was I going, Officer?'
> 'I'd say about 90.'
> 'Suppose you get down off that motorcycle and give me a ticket.'
> 'Suppose I give you a warning instead.'
> 'Suppose it doesn't take.'
> 'Suppose I have to rap you over the knuckles.'
> 'Suppose I bust out crying and put my head on your shoulder.'
> 'Suppose you put it on my husband's shoulder.'
> Pause. A look from Walter. 'That tears it.'

But nothing is torn. They are hooked instead. And so is the audience.

One could, indeed, go on and on quoting the dialogue of Walter Neff and Phyllis Dietrichson. When he returns a few days later, she apologizes for breaking an earlier date but he deflects her with a blithe, 'I was working on my stamp collection.' A little later things get a bit tougher when he accuses her of what she still refuses to admit, that she wants to enlist him in a plan to take out accident insurance on her husband without his knowing it, kill him and collect on the policy:

'His attraction to her is too strong'

'Boy, what a dope you must think I am.'
'I think you're rotten.'
'I think you're swell – as long as I'm not your husband.'

This really should have torn it. But hours later, in his apartment, he reflects that of course it did not. His attraction to her is too strong. And she knows it. When she rings his doorbell a few minutes later, he knows it is her before he answers the door. After another few wary moments they embrace, and her perfume arouses him. What is it? he asks.

'I don't know, I bought it in Ensenada.'
'We ought to have some of that pink wine to go with it. All I've got is bourbon.'
'Bourbon will be fine, Walter.'

That last is a sublime touch. He would clearly like to convert the rutting impulse into a romantic one. She, just as clearly, only wants to get on with this phase of her job, and will accept any instrument, however

Stanwyck and MacMurray shooting at a Los Angeles supermarket in wartime, the shelves groaning with food and guarded by members of the L.A.P.D.

blunt, that will aid her – including plebeian booze. The reference to Ensenada is, by the way, equally on the mark. It was, and is, a resort just over the Mexican border, which in those days featured a casino and catered to a fast crowd that was not quite the right crowd in Los Angeles.

The speed and brightness of this crosstalk lift some of the darkness off what would otherwise be an unbearably black tale. It also tells us something interesting about Walter Neff, especially when we contrast it with the somber self-awareness of his voice-over monologue. After all, this is a man who, as he drives away from his first encounter with Phyllis, acknowledges not only his fatal sexual attraction, but his knowledge that, hopeless in its thrall, he will aid and abet her dark scheme. 'It was a hot afternoon, and I can still remember the smell of honeysuckle all along that street. How could I have known murder can sometimes smell like honeysuckle?' Later, having done the deed, he takes a midnight walk and begins to reflect that, perfect as their crime seems, 'Everything could go wrong.' At which point he also realizes, 'I couldn't hear my own footsteps. It was the walk of a dead man.'

No, this is not a stupid man. Untutored, of course, but not stupid. One thinks back to Joe Sistrom's aphorism: 'All the characters in B pictures are too smart.' It would apply uncomfortably to Walter if the spirit of his interior monologue were carried over into his dialogue. Indeed, that spirit carried over into his daily dealings would have prevented him from becoming involved with Phyllis Dietrichson. But his exchanges with her, with everyone, reveal him to be a man who has allowed himself, perhaps schooled himself, to be just a little too smooth, a little too quick, a little too salesman-sleazy. It has helped him to get on in the world, but it has also left him vulnerable to it: to Phyllis's anklet and her cheap Ensenada perfume, and, as important, to the notion that after eleven years in the insurance game, he knew enough about industry procedures to scam his own company far more successfully than an outsider, an amateur, could:

> Because you know how it is, Keyes. In this business you can't sleep for figuring out all the things they can pull on you. You're like the guy behind the roulette wheel, watching the customers to

> make sure they don't crook the house, and then one night you get to thinking you could crook the house yourself, and do it smart, because you've got the wheel under your hand, you know every notch in it by heart.

This is an adaptation, and a handsome polishing, of Cain's paragraph on the subject, the one that revealed, incidentally, his inspiration for the story – which was not, as so many commentators have thought, the Ruth Snyder-Judd Grey murder of her husband, one of the tabloid sensations of the 1920s. It was rather an anecdote Arthur Krock told Cain about a newspaper proof-reader whose sole job was to prevent salacious typographical errors from creeping into his paper. Having devoted his life to this job, there came a night when he could no longer resist letting a howler, set in headline type, past – and damn the consequences. And he was a better, stronger man than Walter Neff.[11]

That made a perfectly plausible – and to Wilder and Chandler, as to Cain, an agreeably ironic – psychological turning point for their insurance man. The problem with Cain's work was an unpersuasively over-plotted conclusion and his improbable characterization of Phyllis's motives. The two flaws are related.

Up to Dietrichson's murder, the film follows Cain's plot quite closely. It is a complicated business, and a bit of a strain on credulity, but it is also pretty much a MacGuffin, not to be dwelled upon unduly. As both novella and film tell it, Walter lurks unobserved – that's the difficult point to believe – in the back seat of the car when Phyllis drives her husband to the railroad depot where he plans to board a train taking him to his college reunion. On a dark street she stops, Walter kills him and then impersonates him, boarding the train and riding on it for a few miles. At a prearranged point he jumps off the observation car, she meets him, and they place her husband's body on the tracks so that it appears he jumped, fell or was pushed from the train.

After that, however, novella and film diverge. Cain had worked out a complicated back story in which Phyllis, a nurse, turns out to have been a mass murderer, the killer not only of her husband's first wife, but of several children placed in her care. In his story a character named Zachetti, supposed to be the lover of Phyllis's stepdaughter Lola, is actually the vengeful son of a physician who was blamed for Phyllis's

Overleaf: Placing the body on the tracks

earlier crimes. In his effort to gather evidence against the older woman he becomes her lover. When Phyllis and Walter arrange a tryst in Griffith Park, where each plans to do in the other, Zachetti and Lola, also in the park as the result of some rather desperate authorial manoeuvrings, are implicated in the wounding of Walter, and, as a result, are accused of Lola's father's murder by the insurance investigator, Keyes. It is in order to save Lola from a police third degree that Walter confesses his part in the murder to Keyes.

This is not good plotting: it requires too much exposition. It is especially tedious if you have to try to dramatize it on film. So Wilder and Chandler cleared out the underbrush. They let Phyllis's murder of the first Mrs Dietrichson stand. And they allowed Walter to fall in love with Phyllis's stepdaughter; it's a nice irony, and besides, she's the film's only truly innocent party, a refreshing note in these proceedings. As for Zachetti, he is presented as an angry juvenile delinquent, making love to both women (and, of course, cheating on both of them), but conspiring with Phyllis to enlist Walter's expertise in their plan to rid themselves of her inconvenient husband. After which, as Walter comes to realize, he will be next. Except that, of course, he discovers their scheme and comes to Phyllis's house planning to murder her in such a way that Zachetti gets the blame. That plan is spoiled only because she shoots and wounds him before he kills her, which, in turn, sets up his dying confession.

The Wilder–Chandler replotting simplifies everything. It is moved by the most basic emotions – greed and lust. It requires very little in the way of complicated explanation. And it somehow suits the milieu of the movie. One thinks that Los Angeles in some way encourages the blend of complicated plotting and simplified motivation on display here. It is so like – well, the movies as they make them there.

If Wilder and Chandler's work has a disadvantage it is that it denies Phyllis her exculpatory madness. But Cain handled that very poorly. He has her as a creature in love with death. She even has a bridal gown, a red, sleeveless shroud, which she dons whenever she contemplates consummation of a union with her one true love. In the midst of what is otherwise a naturalistic fiction this reads almost laughably in its awkward pretentiousness. And it leads, literally, to a bad ending, in which Keyes lets Walter and Phyllis slip away from the law, but arranges for them to end up together on a cruise ship where, the last we hear of them, they are preparing to commit suicide by slipping over the side in shark-infested waters. How much better the movie's conclusion.

The final confrontation between Walter and Phyllis is masterful – simple, direct, yet rich with overtone. She shoots and wounds him; he advances on her with intent to kill; she tries one more time to seduce him, admitting that she never loved him, until – of all things! – this very moment.

> Sorry, Baby, I'm not buying.
> I'm not asking you to buy. Just hold me.

He does. And then comes the movie's highest moment: a sudden widening of her eyes as she feels his revolver press into her side; there's a beat; he says, 'Goodbye, Baby'; and we hear a shot. It is among the most persuasively realistic violent deaths in movie history, marvelously understated by the director and the actors; surely it is the most unforgettable.

'The movie's highest moment'

The film's coda is equally fine, although, as we will see, it was not arrived at easily. It occurs after Walter has finished talking himself to death, his unattended wound leaking his life-blood away as he dictates. Very simply, it permits Neff a gentle, almost wistful end after all his desperate exertions. Like the conclusion of a Hitchcock movie it restores order to the disordered universe of the movie, and it does so lightly, rightly.

Though the scene was not imagined or written until shooting on the picture was well along, it is the logical conclusion to some of the best work Wilder and Chandler did on the script, which was to expand the character of the claims investigator, Barton Keyes, and enrich his relationship with Neff. In Cain's story, we vaguely understand the demon claims investigator to be a sort of father figure to Walter. But he is a distant and somewhat menacing one. In the movie their relationship is much warmer, and it is set forth in much richer detail. 'It's the love story in the picture,' as Wilder put it. He was not exaggerating.

In retrospect the idea of having Neff, after dispatching Phyllis (and thus discharging, at last, his perverse impulses), find peace by dying in the comforting company of Keyes seems inevitable. But it

 Walter's 'cheap trick'

would not have occurred if Wilder and Chandler had not worked so hard and so carefully to make Keyes a full-scale character. In the film, Keyes becomes an amusingly awkward, deliciously obsessed figure. He has 'a little man' inside him, a tiny imaginary creature who thrashes around uncontrollably – there is not enough Bromo-Seltzer in the world to calm him – when a case arouses his suspicions. This conceit humanizes, renders comical, Keyes's paranoid nature. So does the fact that he is always without matches to light his cigars, a lack Neff is always filling with matches he lights by a flick of his thumbnail – a cheap trick guys like him used to learn, in the days before safety matches, in order to impress girls.

At a point in the film before Walter is too deeply involved with Phyllis, Keyes even offers him a way out, a healthy alternative to his growing sickness. It is a job as his assistant in the claims department, which will allow him to stop being 'a peddler, a glad-hander, a back-slapper'. Even if the pay is less, Keyes argues, it is man's work he's offering, smart man's work:

> A desk job, that's all you can see in it, just a hard chair to park your pants on from nine to five, just a pile of paper to shuffle around, five sharp pencils, and a scratch pad to do some figures on – maybe a little doodling on the side. Well, that's not the way I look at it. To me a claimsman is a surgeon and that desk is an operating table. And those pencils are scalpels and bone chisels. And those papers are not just forms and statistics and claims for compensation. They're alive, they're packed with drama, with busted hopes and crooked dreams. A claimsman is a doctor and a bloodhound and a cop and a judge and a jury and a father confessor . . .

Yes, definitely the latter. But Neff's phone rings in the midst of this impassioned speech, Keyes interrupts to answer, and finds it's 'some dame' named Margie. 'Bet she drinks from the bottle,' he sneers – he's a lifelong bachelor who broke his only engagement when he could not resist investigating his fiancée and discovered she was not all she pretended to be. When Walter finishes his call and turns Keyes down, the older man can't hide his disappointment. 'I thought you were a shade less dumb than the rest of this outfit. Guess I was wrong. You're not smarter, just taller.'

It's a grand actor's moment for Edward G. Robinson, but this scene is something more than that. It is the annunciation of Keyes as the figure Cain could never bring himself to write, the on-site moral chorister for this story, its Philip Marlowe, if you will. Once the claimsman is firmly situated in that role, there is no way for the literal-minded to condemn this film for 'immorality' or even amorality.

Something else happens in this moment, too. When we see Neff through Keyes's eyes we see that he has some redeeming virtue, hidden from himself, hidden from us until this moment. Until then, we have read him as no more than a wise guy, a man of no depth or substance. Keyes's reading of him grants Neff redeeming possibilities. Anyway, a redeeming ambiguity. And it grants the picture a slight air of suspense. It is always possible, one thinks, that Neff might find in himself the will to resist the scheming Phyllis. The scene also, of course, establishes Keyes's ferocity; we see why Neff is afraid of him. And we also see why he must challenge Keyes. If he can outsmart him in a game of wits, the only father shiftless Walter Neff has apparently ever known will be surpassed, and he will become at last the man he aspires to be. Or perhaps one should say, *might* have aspired to had he been blessed with the self-awareness that comes to him only belatedly in this narrative.

Or so we may fairly speculate. The movie is too smart to insist on such crude psychologizing. It just hints at it and moves on. In much the same way it hints that Walter has fallen in love with Lola, its only other admirable figure, but does not permit him to admit that, either.

All along, the film makes these subtle improvements on the original material. In Cain, Phyllis's husband is presented neutrally. In the picture he is a crabby, impatient man on whom we waste no distracting sympathy when he is dispatched. In Cain, the only person who could possibly identify Neff as the man on the train is merely mentioned. In the movie he appears as a talkative hick from Medford, Oregon, so bemused by the importance this case grants him (and the expense account the insurance company is paying him to help in its investigation) that he fails to recognize Neff when he is close enough to touch him. It makes for a lovely scene, at once edgy and funny.

That is the way of this masterfully crafted screenplay. By cleaning up the storyline, particularly in its latter half, it grants Cain's work the narrative cohesiveness and psychological coherence it distinctly lacked.

By giving Neff outs that he does not take, it increases both the irony and the suspense of the story and grants him a complexity and a sympathy he was missing originally. By developing Keyes, and by giving all the minor figures qualities that actors can play and audiences can amuse themselves with, it lifts the oppressiveness from Cain's work, allowing it (and us) to breathe a little more comfortably. Yet at no time does it betray the gloomy vision of human nature that underlay the novelist's work. In the long, mostly dismal history of 'opening up' stories thought to be too confined either physically or psychologically for cinematic exposition, no one has ever done a more delicately artful job than these writers did. Indeed, in the long history of literary adaptation, it is hard to think of a screenplay that more markedly improved on its source, simultaneously eradicating its flaws and granting it nuances unimagined by its original author.

4

There were executives at Paramount who did not believe that Wilder would ever 'lick' *Double Indemnity*. Indeed, they had in hand, before he and Chandler began work, a letter from the Breen office roundly disapproving Cain's novella, and it speaks well of them – or perhaps of Wilder's growing clout on the lot – that they permitted him to go to script on the project.

Among other things, the Breen office missive condemned the piece for permitting Walter Neff to demonstrate redeeming qualities, and added: 'The general low tone and sordid flavor makes it, in our judgement, thoroughly unacceptable for screen presentation.' When they read the finished script, however, the censors were reduced to nit-picking. Be sure Phyllis's bath towel fully covers her, they warned. Don't go into too many details about the disposition of the murdered corpse. Eliminate a line in which Walter tells Phyllis not to handle the insurance policy on her husband unless she is wearing gloves. (As Gerald Gardner comments in *The Censorship Papers*, they reasoned that 'if they could conceal the method by which life is reproduced among mammals they could conceal the method of identifying felons by their fingerprints.'[12]

Overleaf: Tom Powers (centre) as Phyllis's husband

The piddling nature of these comments is, of course, a tribute to the art of the screenwriters. They were naturally conscious of the dangerous ground they were treading with the code administrators. But they saw that the issues that had exercised the censors before the fact were essentially aesthetic, not moral. It was not so much what Cain had said, but the way he said it, blunt and artless, that made *Double Indemnity* look so dangerous to moralists. By attacking what they saw as legitimate problems, Wilder and Chandler obviated the less legitimate ones. Lightening and brightening the story with their dialogue, adding the 'love story' between Neff and Keyes, removing the psychopathic overtones from Phyllis's character – all these things, good in themselves, had the further effect of disarming the censors.

This cannot have been an unintended consequence; Wilder is too intelligent, too shrewdly manipulative, for one to believe that. But one does have the sense with this movie, as with so many good movies, that some of its success was serendipitous, that the right people happened to engage with the right material at just the right moment. Indeed, it may be that for once even the censors lent a helping creative hand. For the Breen office's one large remaining objection to the finished script was that its concluding sequence, which takes place in the death house when Neff is executed for his crime, was 'unduly gruesome'. This was merely a warning, not a proscription, but it clearly worked on Wilder as he shot the film, and his response to it, as well as to the promptings of his own sensibility, greatly improved the picture he finally placed in release.

Certainly, good luck attended *Double Indemnity*'s casting. Barbara Stanwyck raised some initial objections to the role. The child of a broken home, raised by various foster parents, she had begun working as a chorus girl on Broadway when she was an adolescent, and in her early years on the screen she had played plenty of lower-class women struggling to raise themselves in status. One of the best of her early films, *Baby Face*, in which she plays a young woman who had been sexually abused while growing up and then revenges herself on the entire male sex as she sleeps her way upward from filing clerk to board chairman's mistress in a Wall Street bank, was almost a rehearsal for the ruthlessness she would be required to display as Phyllis Dietrichson. Lately, though, she had been playing, in general,

Barbara Stanwyck in *Lady of Burlesque* (1943)

somewhat classier roles and she hesitated over this part. Still, she had done *Ball of Fire* and more recently she had played a stripteaser in *Lady of Burlesque*, a role several other great ladies of the screen had disdained. Besides, she knew a good part when she saw one. 'Are you an actress or a mouse?' Wilder asked her. Or words to that effect.

And so she signed on, not knowing, surely, what is now quite clear to us: that she was about to create one of the enduring archetypes of the American screen, the *noir* female. Certainly this creature had her antecedents in the vamps of the silent screen. But they tended to be European in origin, and to hide their schemings under a highly romantic manner. It might also be argued that there were hints of what was to come in figures like Mary Astor's Brigid O'Shaughnessy in *The Maltese Falcon* (though she, of course, affected a genteel disguise for her true motives). But really the bluntness and hardness of Stanwyck's work was something essentially new, and the alacrity with which it was imitated in film after film of the 40s is one of the interesting, largely unexplored questions of our movie and social history. It surely had something to do with the freedom American women claimed for themselves during the war years, and the nervousness that stirred among males – especially males who were absent at the front and concerned about the fidelity of the girls they left behind. Hard to keep them down on the farm (or behind a suburban picket fence) after they had found work in the rough atmosphere of factories, known the joys of living alone and, for that matter, going to bars alone. Phyllis Dietrichson did none of those things, but she had been a working woman and she was clearly capable of – putting it mildly – a high degree of self-sufficiency.

George Raft, of all people, had been the first choice to play opposite Stanwyck. But he proved, as he so often did, a much harder case to sign on. For dim, actorish reasons he had turned down *High Sierra* and *The Maltese Falcon*, thereby permitting Humphrey Bogart to emerge from character parts to authentic stardom. Now he was telling Wilder – it's an anecdote the director cherishes and has often repeated – he wouldn't do Walter Neff unless the part was rewritten. 'Where's the lapel?' he asked Wilder. What lapel? You know, when the guy flips his lapel over and shows his badge. Meaning, of course, that he had been a good guy all along. Wilder regretfully informed Raft that he contemplated no such switcheroos in *Double Indemnity*. 'No lapel, no George Raft,' came the reply.

Brian Donlevy said essentially the same thing. At which point Wilder had pretty much run through Paramount's roster of tough guys. But then he had an inspiration. Why not a soft guy – a soft guy pretending to be tough? Why not, say, Fred MacMurray? Everyone thought he was crazy. The man had been a saxophone player in an orchestra when talent scouts spotted him. He had been a likeable juvenile since 1934, a second-tier Paramount star no one thought of as any sort of actor. Including Fred MacMurray. He said as much to Wilder when the director approached him. But Wilder persisted, constantly importuning the actor. 'Day after day I retreated, shaking my head,' MacMurray later recalled. 'I didn't want to admit that I was refusing the part because I was afraid of it, because I feared that a guy who had played nothing but comedy roles would find this part too heavy to handle.'[13]

Wilder knew what he was doing. 'I wanted a decent, bourgeois man,' Wilder said recently. But there was something so wonderfully slippery about his performance, somebody said. 'I didn't say he sang in a church choir,' Wilder replied. 'That was a dance band he played in.' Meaning that MacMurray inevitably knew something about the hard and slippery side of life – one-night stands, shady nightclubs, wise guy managers – a life that Walter Neff, sometime vacuum cleaner salesman, full-time bachelor about town, knew.

In other words, MacMurray and Neff were opposite sides of the same coin. The actor was a good man who had been exposed to seamy values. The character he played was a scuzzball, who in some part of his soul – that part that shrewd Barton Keyes could discern and hoped to develop – knew better than to be what he was, do what he did. And physically he was perfect for the part, his size and solidity contrasting so ironically with the psychological insubstantiality he projected. But one must not take anything away from MacMurray's performance technically. It is so wonderfully shifty-eyed. His Neff is always trying to judge his effect on others, always desperately trying to discern their motives, always desperately trying to pretend to be smarter, tougher, quicker than he really is.

His co-stars are wonderful. There is a lonely subtext to

Robinson's bachelor, something needy peeping out from under his bluster, his competence, his implacability, that is very touching. And the note of fraudulence in Stanwyck's sexuality is marvelously judged. Her heat never quite removes the chill in the air when she's around. But both these actors had been here before. MacMurray never had, and he would have only two chances to return to it – as Kiefer, the sneaky intellectual who foments *The Caine Mutiny* and, of course, as the corrupt corporate executive, Jeff Sheldrake, in Wilder's *The Apartment*. ('You're not going to do this to me again,' he told Wilder when he offered him that part, for he had, at the time, a contract at Disney where he was to play clean, upstanding American idiots; but he could not resist another chance at greatness.) His is, I think, one of the greatest performances in the history of American movies. And, because he remains typed in everyone's mind as just another agreeable face, the least acknowledged of them. He was not even nominated for an Academy Award for *Double Indemnity*, or for his two other great performances.

Shooting, which took less than two months (September 27 to November 24) in 1943, went well, that is to say serendipitously. Many years later Wilder would remember with pleasure cameraman John

 The right atmosphere: Phyllis's Spanish-style home

Seitz's discovery of how to create the right atmosphere in Phyllis's Spanish-style home. 'Those houses always looked dusty to me,' he said, and there is actually a line in the script to nail the point home. What Seitz did was fill the air with finely ground aluminium filings. It reflected sunlight from the windows, so the camera could read these particles as it could not read the real thing. Wilder recalled having one of his old bachelor digs at the Chateau Marmont recreated for Neff's apartment, and it has just the right transient air, impersonal, not quite lived-in. His location shooting was similarly inspired. There was not a lot of it, but it was very judiciously placed in the film. A bowling alley, a drive-in, a grocery store, the exterior of the Dietrichson house – there was something isolated, unwelcoming about all of them. Oh yes, Billy Wilder knew something in his bones about being rootless in Los Angeles.

He also knew when to take advantage of an accident. One morning he finished, or so he thought, the little nothing of a scene in which Walter and Phyllis, having disposed of her husband's body, start her car and head home. He broke for lunch, and went to pick up his own car in order to drive to the Brown Derby. When he got in, he

'Halted by a faulty ignition'

found it wouldn't start. He leapt out and started running back across the lot to his stage, praying the grips had not yet dismantled the set. Luckily, they had not. Wilder ordered retakes in which the murderers, desperate to make a quick getaway, are momentarily, suspensefully, halted by a faulty ignition.

MacMurray thought the character was going too far with it. The car was just a mock-up on a rear-projection stage and the actors had to pantomime their business – there was literally no dashboard, no ignition key or switch. Wilder kept extending their business, and MacMurray kept objecting, saying the scene could not hold for the length Wilder was insisting on. But it did. The nothing scene was suddenly something.

Wilder's worries were mostly small. Stanwyck's blonde wig, for instance. Was it just a bit too much, a tad over the top? It's a question devotees of the film still debate as earnestly as Wilder did on his sleepless nights. There was the question of whether the film needed one more hot sexual encounter between Walter and Phyllis, something that would prove the depths of his enthrallment. That was not such a small matter. Aside from the problems such a scene might have made with the

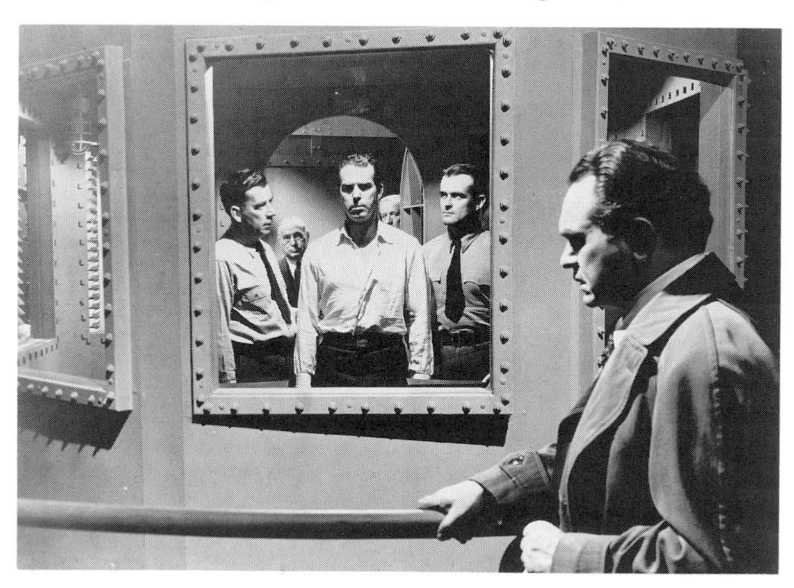

Fred MacMurray and Edward G. Robinson in the execution scene, which was cut from the film as released

Breen office, and the technical problem of staging it persuasively, given the restrictions the censors imposed on all such scenes, there is another issue. Phyllis was a fantasy as well as a reality, and the haste and perfunctory quality of their love scenes help keep Walter on the string. If he had possessed her fully, would he have been so eager to carry out their murder plot? Wasn't it necessary to keep her promise distant, a reward for services rendered? Remember, too, that Phyllis was herself in love with Zachetti (although neither Walter nor the audience is aware of that until later) and so naturally inclined to a certain reserve in her relationship with Walter. And, finally, all of that leaves her basic bitchiness out of the account. Again, this adds up to a nice, endlessly debatable point.

What seems indisputable is the correctness of Wilder's decision to cut the script's concluding death-house sequence, even though it was shot – at a cost said to be $150,000 – and even though the director has frequently called it one of the best scenes he's ever made. In description, however, it sounds lugubrious, too weighty for a film that, despite its dark subject matter, is always light on its feet. To Wilder, Neff was 'a victim, not a murderer', and it seemed wrong to emphasize, as the execution scene did, his criminality.

This problem obviously nagged at him as exposed film kept piling up, and it is difficult to say when exactly the happiest and most important inspiration of his shoot occurred to Wilder. He did mention the wail of distant police sirens on the soundtrack when, Neff having finished his dictation and Keyes having appeared to overhear the last of it, Neff attempts to make an escape. To Wilder's ear the sirens had a ring of finality.

This implies that he was looking at a rough cut of the scene, with temporary sound effects dubbed in, when the idea of concluding the picture with a final, tender, redemptive moment between the two friends occurred to him. But whenever it came to him, it was a great idea, and it required only a little writing and shooting to execute. Apparently the script always proposed that Neff should get up to go, announcing that he's heading for the border, as well as Keyes's rejoinder: 'You'll never make it to the elevator.'

He is correct. All that it was necessary for Wilder to do was to follow Neff to the glass front doors of his office, where he collapses, and then have Keyes join him there. The new material that follows could not have been simpler. As Neff lies there, expiring, he gropes for a cigarette and a match. Reversing the business that has defined their relationship throughout the picture, Keyes strikes the match for his friend. Now Neff cannot resist chiding Keyes for not being able to see what was right before his eyes: 'The guy you were looking for was right across the desk from you.' 'Closer than that,' Keyes says sadly. 'I love you, too,' Neff replies, his last words an attempt at a wisecrack. But also an attempt at the truth. In short, he dies as he lived, a mixed-up guy.

At least he dies in the right arms, though, within the relationship he should not have spurned, within a circle of light, contrasting vividly with the darkness that has closed more and more tightly around him ever since his first meeting with Phyllis.

5

As *Double Indemnity* moved through post-production heading toward release in the autumn of 1944, it became Hollywood's most talked

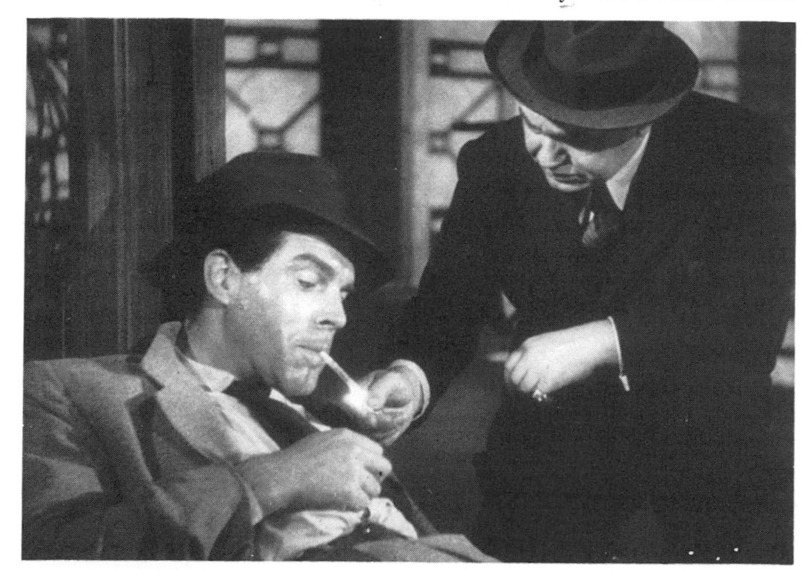

'I love you, too.'

about, most eagerly awaited film. Obviously the technicians working on it, and the studio executives screening it, recognized that the film was not quite like any that had gone before it, and that within the new terms it set it was brilliantly made.

Includin its score, which was the most important element added to the picture in post-production. Indeed, it is crucial to the whole effect. Artfully repetitive, it is insinuating rather than overpowering – a kind of nervous buzzing in the strings, edgy and 'neurotic' (to borrow the term Vincente Minnelli used to describe the great, delirious waltz the same composer, Miklos Rosza, wrote for his *Madame Bovary* five years later). It is as unnerving, as dislocating, as the picture itself proved to be.

Some of the film's initial power may have been the result of another lucky break – the timing of its release. One has to think that in this wartime period the contrast between *Double Indemnity*'s hardness of spirit and the sentimental, patriotic pieties in which American movies had been trafficking was just simply refreshing to its first viewers, a slap in the face with a cold towel. In any case, the first preview confirmed the buzz about the film, and banished any lingering doubts Wilder may have entertained about it. The preview was in one of the big theaters in Westwood, and that locale assured that a jury of the director's peers were present.

They were gripped by what they saw. As Wilder says, 'You know very well how a picture is working – it's in their breathing, and their non-breathing.' Walking out of the theater, surrounded by elated co-workers and executives, he spotted Cain, standing quietly, almost hidden by a pillar. He went over to him and was embraced by the writer, who told the director what he later told interviewers, that Wilder had greatly improved his original work.

Talking to Peter Brunette and Gerald Peary, years later, Cain said: 'It's the only picture I ever saw made from my books that had things in it I wish I had thought of. Wilder's ending was much better than my ending, and his device for letting the guy tell the story by taking out the office dictating machine – I would have done it if I had thought of it.' He also loved a moment where Phyllis comes to visit Neff in his apartment only to find Keyes already there, and she has to duck behind the door as he opens it to leave. It 'makes your hand wet',

Cain commented. He approved as well the removal of her 'death trip' and the development of the father-son relationship between Keyes and Neff.

> My story was done very slapdash and very quick – I had to have money. I had made a lot of money, but I had to pay it all out to liquidate a thing that was hanging over my head [a divorce]. I was flat broke ... and the idea for this thing popped into my head. At the end I had the problem of how he and the woman could go off the deep end at the same time and he would leave a diary or something. But the end was not done over enough. All endings to a novel have to be done over and over and over. Christ almighty! You get sick of that last twenty pages![14]

Cain's enthusiasm was echoed everywhere within the business. One of the advertising lines concocted by the marketing department was: '*Double Indemnity* – The Two Most Important Words in the Motion Picture Industry Since *Broken Blossoms*' (a curious association). Playing on it, Alfred Hitchcock, after seeing the film, wired its director: 'Since

 Phyllis behind the door

Double Indemnity the two most important words are Billy Wilder,' and that pretty much summed up the town's reaction. The picture had done for Wilder exactly what he had hoped it would – made him, overnight, a talked about figure, an important film-maker.

Indeed, only Chandler held himself aloof from Hollywood's enthusiasm for *Double Indemnity*, claiming among other things that no one had bothered to invite him to previews or the premiere of a film to which his contribution had been so important. Maybe so, maybe not. He had a tendency to collect and exaggerate injustices, and a little later he wrote a sour, if not entirely inaccurate, essay about the perils of screenwriting, which irritated Wilder, who believed, quite correctly, that Chandler's work on *Double Indemnity* had been treated with high respect, and that the success of the picture had greatly enhanced his salability as a screenwriter, a trade at which Chandler worked quite profitably during the next few years.

Curiously, the industry's sense of the picture's originality and importance did not carry over to the general public. As we have seen, the reviews tended to be tentative, respectful but puzzled, perhaps because reviewers were less aware than the industry of how long the struggle to bring Cain's work to the screen had been, how many pitfalls Wilder had surmounted. And, perhaps then as now, movie journalists were basically reviewing the storyline, slighting the question of cinematic style, which movie people are always more aware of initially than most critics are, since they deal with it in hard, practical terms every day of their lives.

Whatever the case, *Double Indemnity* was not a huge box-office success. It appears nowhere on the list of 1944's top grossers, and although it did not lose money, it did not make much either. Undaunted, Wilder's colleagues in the Motion Picture Academy showered the film with Oscar nominations, and Wilder went off with high hopes to the award ceremonies, which were held at Grauman's Chinese Theater on March 15, 1945. In his judgment the competition for best picture was not particularly strong, and though he was up against the likes of Hitchcock, Otto Preminger and Leo McCarey in the directing category, he thought he had a good chance there too.

He reckoned without his own studio, which had a major commercial success in McCarey's *Going My Way*, a ghastly, sentimental comedy about a young priest (Bing Crosby) and an old priest (Barry Fitzgerald) bickering their way toward a state of grace in their rundown parish. In those days, studios encouraged block voting by their employees in the Academy races, and it was pushing them hard to vote for McCarey's film. It still had life left in it at the box office, whereas *Double Indemnity* was by now played off.

As he recalls the evening Wilder was sitting on the aisle toward the front of the auditorium, with McCarey sitting well behind him on the same aisle. When his name was called out as winner of the best screenplay award, for which Wilder and Chandler were also nominated, McCarey got up quite a head of steam as he rushed down the aisle to claim his prize. The same joyous haste propelled him stageward when he was named best director. By the time Ingrid Bergman had beaten Stanwyck for the best acting prize, Wilder knew this was not his night. And sure enough, here came McCarey again, hurtling down the aisle to collect the best picture Oscar. Cut now to 1991. An 85-year-old Billy Wilder is sitting in his one-room office in Beverly Hills ('If I'd made *Home Alone* it would be a suite') recalling the moment. 'Look at my foot,' he commands. His interviewer does so. It cants outward just a few inches – just as it did on that March night forty-six years previously, just enough to be missed by a rival with his eye on a prize.

Wilder smiles contentedly. 'Mr McCarey ... stumbled perceptibly,' he says. He does not add that thereafter the once-great comedy director stumbled perceptibly in his career. Or that, launched by *Double Indemnity*'s success, Wilder entered upon the first great phase of his professional life, carrying him onward to *Sunset Boulevard, Some Like It Hot* and the other titles indelibly associated with his name. Nor does he quote the remark reputed to him as he left the ceremony: 'What the hell does the Academy Award mean, for godsake? After all, Luise Rainer won it two times.' He prefers instead to note that there is a rough justice in these matters, that a year later he was rushing to the stage, claiming his own best picture and best director prizes for *The Lost Weekend*.

That was, of course, a good and important film, the first movie to treat alcoholism as a disease, and a gritty, realistic piece of film-making. It may be, as he implies, that some of the votes for it were actually belated votes for *Double Indemnity*. It is certain, in any case, that neither it nor any other film Wilder made has had *Double Indemnity*'s influence on the history of American movies. It is equally certain that no film he ever made has a larger claim on our regard. Or on his own. Wilder once said it was his favorite film. Asked to explain himself he said simply: 'It has the fewest mistakes.' And that, probably, is as good a place as any to rest the case for this daring and masterful movie.

NOTES

1 Eric Lax, *Woody Allen*. New York: Alfred A. Knopf, 1991, pp. 37–8.
2 James Agee, *The Nation*, 14 October 1944, reprinted in James Agee, *Agee on Film*. New York: McDowell-Obolensky, 1958.
3 Bosley Crowther, '"Double Indemnity", a Tough Melodrama, With Stanwyck and MacMurray as Killers, Opens at the Paramount', *New York Times*, 7 September 1944, reprinted in George Amberg (ed.), *The New York Times Film Reviews, 1913–1970*. New York: Arnow Press/Quadrangle, 1971, pp. 119–20.
4 Alain Silver and Elizabeth Ward (eds.), *Film Noir: An Encyclopedic Reference to the American Style*. Woodstock, N.Y.: Overlook Press, 1979, Appendix B.
5 Edmund Wilson, 'The Boys in the Back Room', in Edmund Wilson, *Classics and Commercials*. New York: Farrar, Straus, 1950, pp. 19–22. All subsequent quotations from Wilson are drawn from this essay.
6 Roy Hoopes, *Cain*. Carbondale and Edwardsville, Ill.: Southern Illinois University Press, 1982, p. 332.
7 Stephen Farber, 'The Films of Billy Wilder', *Film Comment*, vol. 7, no. 4, Winter 1971–2.
8 Quoted in Frank MacShane, *The Life of Raymond Chandler*. New York: E. P. Dutton, 1976, p. 101.
9 Peter Brunette and Gerald Peary, 'James M. Cain: Tough Guy', in Pat McGilligan (ed.), *Backstory: Interviews with Screenwriters of Hollywood's Golden Age*. Berkeley, Los Angeles, London: University of California Press, 1986, p. 127.
10 Ibid., p. 126.
11 Roy Hoopes, *Cain*, p. 258.
12 Gerald Gardner, *The Censorship Papers: Movie Censorship Letters from the Hays Office, 1934 to 1968*. New York: Dodd, Mead, 1987, pp. 44–7.
13 Roy Hoopes, *Cain*, p. 335.
14 Peter Brunette and Gerald Peary, in *Backstory*, pp. 125–6.

CREDITS

Double Indemnity

USA
1944
Production company
Paramount Pictures
US release
7 September 1944
Distributor (US)
Paramount
UK release
16 October 1944
Distributor (UK)
Paramount
Copyright date
21 April 1944
Executive producer
B. G. DeSylva
Associate producer
Joseph Sistrom
Director
Billy Wilder
Assistant director
C. C. Coleman
Dialogue director
Jack Gage
Screenplay
Billy Wilder, Raymond Chandler from the novel *Double Indemnity* by James M. Cain, published in *Three of a Kind* (1943)
Photography (black and white)
John Seitz
Music
Miklos Rozsa, based on César Franck's Symphony in D minor
Song
'Tangerine' by Victor Schertzinger, Johnny Mercer
Supervising editor
Doane Harrison
Art direction
Hans Dreier, Hal Pereira
Set decorator
Bertram Granger
Costumes
Edith Head
Makeup
Wally Westmore
Process photography
Farciot Edouart
Sound recorders
Stanley Cooley, Walter Oberst
107 minutes
9663 feet

Fred MacMurray
Walter Neff
Barbara Stanwyck
Phyllis Dietrichson
Edward G. Robinson
Barton Keyes
Porter Hall
Mr Jackson
Jean Heather
Lola Dietrichson
Tom Powers
Mr Dietrichson
Byron Barr
Nino Zachetti
Richard Gaines
Edward S. Norton Jr
Fortunio Bonanova
Sam Gorlopis
John Philliber
Joe Peters
Betty Farrington
Nettie the maid
George Magrill
Man
Bess Flowers
Norton's secretary
Kernan Cripps
Redcap
Harold Garrison
Redcap
Oscar Smith
Pullman porter
Constance Purdy
Woman
Dick Rush
Pullman conductor
Frank Billy Mitchell
Pullman porter
Edmund Cobb
Train conductor
Floyd Shackleford
Pullman porter
James Adamson
Pullman porter
Sam McDaniel
Charlie, garage attendant
Clarence Muse
Man
Judith Gibson
Pacific All-Risk telephone operator
Miriam Franklin
Keyes's secretary
Douglas Spencer
Lou Schwartz

(Roles in execution chamber scene, cut from release print)
Alan Bridge
Execution chamber guard
Edward Hearn
Warden's secretary
George Anderson
Warden
George Melford
Doctor
Lee Shumway
Door guard
William O'Leary
Chaplain
Boyd Irwin
Doctor

Double Indemnity was remade for television in 1973, directed by Jack Smight, screenplay by Steven Bochco, with Richard Crenna as Walter Neff, Lee J. Cobb as Barton Keyes and Samantha Eggar as Phyllis Dietrichson.

The print of *Double Indemnity* in the National Film Archive derives from material deposited by Paramount Pictures in 1946.

BIBLIOGRAPHY

Agee, James. *Agee on Film* (New York: McDowell-Obolensky, 1958).

Brunette, Peter and Peary, Gerald. 'James M. Cain: Tough Guy', in Pat McGilligan (ed.), *Backstory: Interviews with Screenwriters of Hollywood's Golden Age* (Berkeley, Los Angeles, London: University of California Press, 1986).

Cain, James M. 'Paradise', *American Mercury*, March 1933, in Roy Hoopes (ed.), *60 Years of Journalism by James M. Cain* (Bowling Green, Ohio: Bowling Green State University Popular Press, 1985).

Crowther, Bosley. '"Double Indemnity", a Tough Melodrama, With Stanwyck and MacMurray as Killers, Opens at the Paramount'. *New York Times*, 7 September 1944, in George Amberg (ed.), *The New York Times Film Reviews, 1913–1970* (New York: Arnow Press/Quadrangle, 1971).

Farber, Stephen. 'The Films of Billy Wilder', *Film Comment*, vol. 7, no. 4, Winter 1971–2.

Gardner, Gerald. *The Censorship Papers: Movie Censorship Letters from the Hays Office, 1934 to 1968* (New York: Dodd, Mead, 1987).

Gifford, Barry. *The Devil Thumbs a Ride and Other Unforgettable Films* (New York: Grove Press, 1988).

Hirsch, Foster. *The Dark Side of the Screen: Film Noir* (San Diego, New York: A. S. Barnes, 1981).

Hoopes, Roy. *Cain* (Carbondale and Edwardsville, Ill.: Southern Illinois University Press, 1982).

Lax, Eric. *Woody Allen* (New York: Alfred A. Knopf, 1991).

MacShane, Frank. *The Life of Raymond Chandler* (New York: E. P. Dutton, 1976).

Silver, Alain and Ward, Elizabeth (eds.). *Film Noir: An Encyclopedic Reference to the American Style* (Woodstock, N.Y.: The Overlook Press, 1979).

Wilson, Edmund. 'The Boys in the Back Room', in Edmund Wilson, *Classics and Commercials* (New York: Farrar, Straus, 1950).

Zolotow, Maurice. *Billy Wilder in Hollywood* (New York: Limelight Editions, 1987). (Revised edition of work originally published in 1977.)